AROUND THE CORNER

A Poetry Collection

Jane Criley Denney

Copyright © 2023 Jane Criley Denney. All rights reserved. No part of this book may be used or reproduced in any form without express written permission from the publisher except for brief quotes, approved excerpts, articles, and reviews. For information, quotes from the author, or interview requests. contact the publisher.

Knoxville, Tennessee, USA
crippledbeaglepublishing.com

Cover concept and design by Jane Criley Denney, Marnie Criley, and Jody Dyer

Paperback ISBN 978-1-958533-30-7
Hardcover ISBN 978-1-958533-31-4

Library of Congress Control Number: 2023904257

Printed in the United States of America

Contents

Sweet Peas 9

Feeding the Birds 11

Feeding the Ducks in Centennial Park 12

Galapagos 15

Joy 16

Faces 17

Maple Leaves 18

My Waterfall Quest 19

Learning to Swim at the "Y" 20

String Theory of Everything 21

Little Archie Visits 22

I Name You "Fog" 23

I Give You a Rose 24

Looking Back 25

The Suicide 26

A Mundane Miracle 27

Nation of Strangers? 28

Boundaries 29

October Dream 30

My Unplanned Parents 32

Test Your Knight's Volubility 33

Day Camp 34

To My Husband 36

Medals 38

November Rededication ... 39
Carnival ... 41
God's Love ... 43
Specific Dyslexia ... 44
Waiting at O'Charley's ... 45
The Politician ... 46
Faith ... 47
Ill-Placed Period ... 48
Tears ... 49
Windows ... 50
Trellises ... 51
A Landscaped Mind ... 52
Make Us Whole ... 53
Society ... 54
Box Hockey at West Park ... 56
Summer Flu ... 57
The Death of a Child ... 58
Aunt Dorothy's House ... 60
Kitchen ... 62
A Christmas Bag ... 64
Vacation? ... 67
Wine? ... 68
Love ... 69
Innocence ... 70
Weeds ... 71
Lament of Lachesis ... 72

Someone's Gift 73
About Jane Criley Denney 75

I dedicate my poems to my daughter Marnie.

Sweet Peas

Around the idle corner of the house
Sweet peas blossomed in a spring surprise.
Behind a row of bricks – a messy patch,
Baby oaks, wild onions, and a tangled thatch
Of prickly vines, disordered to the eyes.
Not nature's wildness but man's unconcern –
Planting the flowers and failing to return
Before he packs and moves down ritual rows.

Easing the wild rose aside, I broke
The juicy stems at several joints.
Leaving the greenest flowers to ripen pink
Domesticated the others in the sink
Before I speared them on the hundred points
Of a flower holder, letting them fall
In their own angled way to decorate the hall –
Unhallowed ritual path we have to take.

The paper flowers climbing up the wall
Nodded to let these new ones grow
Into the nostalgic order of their garden.
My eye absorbed each "Beg your pardon"
As it worked to pull out what it had to know –
Reality from shown imagination.
Mind surprised this comic complication
Saying it's more fun not to tell!

Hastened by this forced encounter
Soon drooping angles in a new riddle
Until they were sadly cast away
Around the idle corner to decay

And ponder what had happened in the middle.
Their mirrored likeness left to challenge fate
A little longer as they decorate
A hall that flashes an eternal spring
A relative reality without bothering.

Feeding the Birds

Avoid the shove and buckle
Laid down by a carpet of starlings.

Slip the latch early.

The morning thrush glissades to his meal
Like a nervous dancer
As anxious as you for the moment of song.

Or robins, relaxed old neighbors
Never imposing their glory as cardinals
Who share their burden of brightness accusingly.

Or hidden in shadows the orchard oriole
Bursts into song as if each new blossom
Unfolds a duo of sly hopes
For a troubled world.

A shrewd reversal –
The French breakfast on invading starlings
Wrapped in bacon and roasted
Tender on toast!

Feeding the Ducks in Centennial Park

I took two children, one was mine
To feed the ducks and feel sunshine.

Mostly fish bobbed up for bread
The ducks were likely too well fed.

The children raced around the edge
Forgetting all their safety pledge.

Suddenly they stopped in place
A woman fishing, face to face.

Though she was odd the children sensed
A common kinship, life unfenced.

Laughing at her stretched story
One big fish caught here in glory.

The big tree by her side for shade
(From someone asking for a license paid?)

I, too, lingered beside the tree
Wondering what she would want from me.

Fear of strangers, one way to hide
A certain kind of selfish pride.

Look for it and you're bound to find
Most of what's wrong in all mankind.

Sooner than I'd care to begin
She asked for a trip to Gallatin.

Casually, not really outright,
A chance to fish at a better sight.

Time for lunch and we went away,
The children were ready, no guilt to stay.

My mind sought refuge in my desire
To bring back a sandwich to spark the fire.

Imperfect love brings a sacrifice
To the alter of its edifice.

Accepted with dignity, mine kept, too.
She said she lived in the distant view.

A high-rise for elderly across the way,
No place with her children for her to stay.

When the lightning flashes on the fourteenth floor,
She walks to the fifth to feel safe once more.

The sound of thunder when you're up so high
Threatens like a thoughtless sky.

Told to raise one blind each day
So they'll know you're well enough to pray!

Nothing for bait 'til she retrieves
Night crawlers scratched from discarded leaves.

Whoops! A tiny fish thrown back
Caught in the middle of a luck duck's quack.

The children laughed till they couldn't see.
So did I, so did she.

She yelled at boaters not to break
Duck eggs on the edge of the island's wake.

Popcorn bought for all to eat
Better fed to ducks for a special treat.

Fishing, not really for food or fun,
But the human bond caught one to one.

Old woman, children and, yes, even me
Casting our hooks expectantly.

The other night I was watching Nature on TV and they were featuring the beautiful birds of paradise on the Island of New Guinea. They were magnificent. It reminded me of a book I read a long time ago about Darwin's visit to the Galapagos Islands where he felt his theories found confirmation. Poor fellow, I think they said he was seasick all the way there.

At about the time I read that book my church was having a craft sale to raise money. I don't remember how I did it, but somehow, I made frames for some old mirrors I had and I added some designs to them, out of material I could mold. Three of them were fairly pretty. I made one for myself that was sort of ugly, but I called it my Galapagos mirror. I must have been trying to capture the vastness and some of the animals I had seen in pictures of the place. When I saw the beautiful birds and mountains on TV it made me go out to the barn and see if I still had that mirror. I did. It inspired me to write this poem.

Galapagos

I'd like to go to the Galapagos,
The animals there caused such a fuss
When Darwin's evolutionary years
Said it took forever to make the tears
And brains that reach to God and heaven,
Instead of the days of the Biblical seven.

There, Darwin came to an explanation
(That many called a condemnation)
For all life's rich diversity,
Excitement, love, adversity,
That make us what we are today.
Maybe God did choose this alternate way.

Joy

If every joy I see
I see it moving away from me.
And though I hold it tight
It moves
The moving out of sight.
Should every joy I touch
My touch be light?

Maybe joys that give
Relive.

Faces

Faces file by faces,
One remembering the next in droll-some deviation.
Lips bow, curve of cheek,
Smartly subtle, the molding of the whole.
Sameness of parts sustains stinging surprises.

Feelings shadowed in quick passing
Shape some closer to the heart,
One expression grasped from the past –
Friends, home, and love filling in the text.
The story widens with the years,
The differences graphically, schematically, hurtfully felt.
The sameness digging in, too, storied, un-cellular conformity.

Screen seen faces bridging in false perfection
In the soul – flattening out the heart in a
Trickle of life's tributary yearnings,
Damming up the face feeler,
The charter of curve courses
All dimensional detector!
Leaving only sigh-timed forays into life's forests,
Darting in and out as advertiser dictates – licking blindly.

Better one face known face to face
One cheek oval love affirmed completely
Radiating sunlike – no half-hidden cheek
Stays hateful in the weakest corner of the glow.

Maple Leaves

Maple leaves strike out in the fall
To speak their piece or not at all.

Losing their sap, the botanists say
Wrinkling, drying, ageing away.

Sensing hoarfrost as bittersweet,
Almost to freezing, from cooling the heat.

Green leaves defiantly blush hues intense,
Orange, yellow, magenta, scarlet brilliance.

Loud flush of feeling before petioles give way
Shouts, "Glory, I've lived!" not, "see I decay."

My Waterfall Quest

The sound came first.
The rushing has a music of its own
Both hard and soft
A symphony for some.

But my quest is visual
Around the corner it explodes
Sun and shadows equally reflected
Then the movement startles
Upsets and finally releases.
Seen but unseen the colors
Sensually mix, mesmerizing.

I stand a little frightened, pulled by
Looking down.
Deliberately looking up I see
The nameless green on either side
Unsuccessfully hiding the stabilizing rock
No movement save the memorial
Wearing away of centuries.

Something awakens in me
Must I decide?
Is it the free-flowing majestic rush I quest?
Or the commanding quiet solitude of stone?
I stand alone, questioning.

Learning to Swim at the "Y"

Greenhoused by this stately dome,
Warm exercised aquatics don
The opaque plastic molded space
Undreamed by any Khan.

Pleasure structured inside pool,
Damp four-year-olds at sniffing school.
A kicking, bobbing experience
In training for competition.
Water comforts its own demands
For teacher pleasing exhibition.

Passing, of course, will all depend
On the chemical deep at the other end.

Some dive in fearless jaunty haste,
The determined follow silent.
One swims and screams with breath to spare
Like all who voice dissent.

I labor with their wildest stroke
Maternalizing on every choke.

In spite of all the roar I hear
Your "help" as soft as dew on skin,
Insistent till you reach your goal,
Requiescat in your winning grin.

I've matched the plowing of your tide
With limb and soul poised over the side.

String Theory of Everything

Are we surrounded by a string
Of quantum quivering between what matters,
Pulled less by gravity than thought?
Newton and Einstein with nothing
To disperse their ashes
When their fire has dwindled
In the sanctity of parallel universities.
The universal left deciding whether to
Cry or laugh at the music of the spheres
Played perhaps by a string quartet.

Little Archie Visits

One salmon poppy!

I examined its sultriness – a poor
Substitute for the three promised
At root planting time,
Maybe more sand.

From the window I saw you, too
Garden explorer
Alone and a little out of your territory.
Ah, the inevitable meeting.

Fuzzy, bright, and low
It begged for your picking full out.

But one to one, its closeness urged
Some new consideration –
Confused, your hand lifted from your squat
Looking around to find yourself –

Old buddies, the cornflowers
Tickling you to laughter as you pass
Promising hundreds of buttons for your bachelor days.

Still, you eye the poppy as you pass,
The seeds of inwardness
Sprouting into cookie hunger –
An enviable escape from the
Complexity of being alone, together.

I Name You "Fog"

Tonight, I un-name you fog
To be there at your Christening.

Were you whispered in fear?
You do muffle all suddenness but the last
Cutting through.

Or quilted into the warmth of love's tenderness?
A palpable extension of the dark –
As soft and close as breath?
An old bride's veil?

Or did you go long unnoticed
Till one silent visit found you named in
Jest's discovery of a familiar friend
Standing in the midst of small talk?

Were you the first mirror of grief?

Were you finger explored
Or reconnoitered?

Were you the gray shawl of magic
Peaking behind curious eyes?

I shroud myself in your history.
It is a comfortable habit
And I know well the pathway home.

I Give You a Rose

A rose frees herself from folded womb
Centrifugally and rests,
All energy spent on loveliness.
Those who bore her sit silent in their common names –
Earth, sun, rain, bush
Giving their glory to her opportunity.

I, too, give her my vitality
As I pluck her and become
The nameless feet
Of her embodied beauty which
Scorning further adornment as useless
Unless invisible to all
But the receiving heart.

Looking Back

Snow escapes downhill with
Rung-less ladders of our slide
Printing fleetness on the curve
Momentum of direct descent.

Our gone-ness
Climbs the shadows
Of the tree's sigh
In the sun's swift light.

The Suicide

No tears at your death!

I weep for you in my stomach
As I try to swallow your humanity and mine.

Ebbing, flowing, no satisfaction, no relief
Just the retching waves to wash it all away.

And still it stays.

Love of beauty, art
Trying to make self perfect
God's beautiful imperfect child.

Failing, ending it all.

A Mundane Miracle

A kitten came meowing at our door
At Christmas when we couldn't be more
Occupied, but we stopped to find
A morsel of some fishy kind.
Our feral friend would soon devour,
Meow for more with all her power.
We felt some guilt I'd have to say
As we encouraged her to stay.
For one of ours "will soon be here"
Who hated cats without a peer.
He chased, threw rocks, and cursed away
At cats in general. Come what may,
It would take a miracle at least
For him to tolerate the beast.
But two more Christmases have past
And Christmas cat is just as fast
When called to come and dine
On the best cat food that we could find.
She sleeps some part of every night
Under <u>his</u> bed not quite out of sight.
Perhaps all miracles start this way –
The mundane look of an ordinary day.
A box that held food for sheep
Held a Babe who would someday reap
A crown of thorns and a stone rolled away.
Miracle of miracles first cradled in a bed of hay.

Nation of Strangers?

Everything to separate,
Fitfully conglomerate.

Are you under thirty-five?
Eighty? Black? Half alive?
Baptist? Jobless? Married twice?
Doctor? Plumber? Treat me nice.
Female? Gay? Imbecile?
Psycho, waiting for the kill?
Making several thousand grand?
Politician take the stand.
Groupie? Manager? Or mother?
Never time to meet your brother.
Government to pay the bill?
If you play the way they will.
Collar blue or collar white?
Make me safe for one more night.
Farmer? Likely you are not.
Gone to city, gone to pot.
Student? Soldier? Union? Bored?
Don't wait up for me oh, Lord!

I am moving far away,
I'll come back another day.

Boundaries

Without much thought I ratify the notion
That my religion separates God from sin.
Control is keeping out or margining in
The boundaries of a unified devotion.
But love beams wavelike in its radiation
And never seems to see where they begin.

October Dream

I come no critic to a dream,
Theater, whatever, let it play.
October's early weather, summer's stay.
Pointing no real direction, it teams
With any treat or reminiscence.
Why try explaining shifts of mind
From now in fall to Christmas kind,
Middle age to early adolescence.
Triggered by some mild billowing
Or lusty gust, it travels,
No maze of trickery unravels,
Curtain blown, morning pillowing.
Color tuned comes on full played
Like tired old movies burst on the screen
The darkened you unseen,
Watching you, Christmas-young arrayed.

Caroling, snow clad, lightly playing
Old songs, snow spice and youthful feet
To delight, season excited, glad to meet
All faces, all doors, never staying
Their flight but moving as the weather.
Lighted snow street valleys an enchanted night,
Reflects each face smiling its own white
Thoughts while snowflakes prance together,
Echoing songs sung as only youth
Or practiced talent dares
Strong voices and clear. It cares
For feeling, tune, and truth.

Afterward the big church gathers all
Offering cocoa's smell to warm the crowd.

Led through darkened sanctuary proud
Of its stained-glass windows tall
We walked proudly in procession.
Electric lighted, the outside bright
Shines through the glass, ethereal light.
God's dawn the promise of a night's inception.
Christ portraits reaching out in color vivid
To center pews in blackness stark
And empty – challenging the timid.

Scoring this scene for innocence
Rerunning it for a seasoned audience,
Anxiously awakening from a daybreak dream, I find
It is playing in a pocket of my mind.

My Unplanned Parents

Doe-eyed Irish elfin father
All round and sound
A clown.
Fairy-footed mother
Misty mini-town.

Dreamless city gates
Opened wide for them.
Soon the fairy blue-eyed vision
Drooped and seemed to dim.

Brown-eyed blarney didn't think
It all was folly
As he briskly
Took the trolley.

Forgot and forested one April,
Worried winter fawned the frown
Of their depression daughter
Analyzing root space up and down.

Test Your Knight's Volubility

He rode upon a moonlight mist
And didn't say a word.
He sighed, she sighed, they dearly kissed
But still no voice was heard.

Two wine-red hearts were poured to one
Through lips that met so eager.
Heart rests on heart when love has won,
The need for words is meager.

Alas, the years do lovers' stalk
And kisses will diminish.
The air is strangely free of talk
From dawn until day's finish.

And as she sits herself ignored
Thoughts loom on this persuasion,
Dear hearts don't test his lips adored
But try his conversation.

Day Camp

A home in the woods for ten.
Two mothers – teachers
Outdoor laughing features,
Almost girls again.

Eight boys halfway on the road
To being men,
Glimpses of it now and then
In their quiet balanced mode.

Vines for boy swinging
Like elves
And trying out knives
For themselves.

Sticks for tables
And whittling and fires,
Avoiding briars
And making cables.

The air up high so blue,
Leaves a contrasting canopy hue,
Full compass choice
Pick your direction
With tools of detection –
Eyes, ears and touch
Say so much
With a little reflection.

We beat our own paths
Over marshes and slopes
Bypassing thickets
Nodding "nopes."

Then circling back
(We would anyway —
Circle that is
The nature books say,
If we're not careful.)
Good to know this inclination
If you stray too far
From your destination.
Pick out landmarks
To straighten your course.

Beauty abounds
In the treasures we've found.
Nature's art shops
As free as toad hops
And mushroom pops.
Stories to tell
Flowers to smell,
All of it swell.

In God's woods for a while
His wind whispers a smile.

To My Husband

Each room must grin
When you walk in

Each step you pace
Feels stroked by grace

Each dawn must glow
To let you know

The newborn day
Needs your okay

Each flower must sigh
To catch your eye

Each bird's new song
Dances you along

Each laugh you roar
Opens one more door

Each star grows bright
For your delight

Each inch you shade
Feels overpaid

Each morsel you chew
Grows sweeter for you

Each heart you bless
Echoes yes, yes, yes

For all is new
When touched by you

Medals

We are running out of medals
For an arm, a leg, an eye.
Hurry, make more medals,
Even more of them will die.

We are running out of medals.
Did you melt them to a gun?
Hurry, make more medals,
Can you spare another son?

We are running out of medals
For a war no one can win.
Yes, they deserve the medals,
Someone else must bear the sin.

November Rededication

The heater barely bending the stiff coldness,
Pulling into the turn lane cars blur past
On the way to jobs – punctuating the dullness
Of a November morning as a recurring blast.
The parking lot is full already.
How do they expect me to find a place?
Contending traffic seems part of a study
Rebuttal – linked in another's lateness – three-legged race.

Up the hospital's steps the wind's slap
Chastened the hurrying and the complaints.
The lives inside a traffic trap
Of needs – suffering, loneliness, unwilled constraints.
Take a morning armful of wholeness,
A living basketful of self – promising a momentum
Of kindness to overcome your faults and impress
On those you serve, relief from total tedium.

The Red Cross Volunteer explores the message
That surrounds the meaning of mankind.
Doubts, loss, hurt, neglect – assuage
Those fears and then to leave behind
A legacy of love. That is their aim.
As they inherit, they also will their deeds
To their children. For they must take the blame
If future fails to listen to each other's needs.

So, you left the beds unmade
And go home with an earned fatigue.
See the babysitter is paid
And settle the latest sibling intrigue.

Or perhaps you cook for only one
And spend some time rethinking the day,
Regretting what you left undone
And what you did that failed some way.

Sometimes you talk for years and no reply,
And when it comes it's your turn not to speak.
Your throat is filled with caring as you try
To shape it into words, however weak.
And you lecture, recruit, watch and wait,
Read a little and smile a lot,
Cry inside at the words they dictate,
Or phone until your voice sounds hot.

But more than future dreams
Or a signaled duty to the past,
More than necessary schemes
And morale boosters that may not last,
There is in all the chairmanships,
Pints of blood and hours of sewing,
Procedures filed, tests, clinic trips,
A deep awareness that in your knowing
Heart, a fulfilled love keeps growing.

Whatever the demands and likely cost,
We act in love, or all is boast.

Carnival

Mutt and Jeff cousins – two he's and my she,
Tall boy, sixteen, in arm with sixish glee.
Younger brother shuffles along, too near
To childhood to grasp its fear
In his hand. His own flaunted
In the roller coaster winds that haunted
Him all the way there in the car.
Thrilling over and over again to prove how far
He had come in one small oval of space,
Up and down so fast to win the race.

One of two mothers, I watched them with pride
Melting in a quick hurt, like the side
Of the hero puppet concaving one big grimace
As he flees from the scary walking on,
A child's pace increases with growth, and he's gone.

Carnival contingency, bring your mood
And see it tightened to a giggle or a brood,
Remembering how other carnivals had ended
Wound so tight the coils contended
The next day, as you try to make
Boredom just be boredom, not an ache.
Now the excitement and the ache are one,
Age a rebellion that must fight for fun.

I see the young ones to spice their life
Prove more belly buttons than a midwife's knife.
Belly buttons looking for their mates
As good as any preening of nature's traits.
Grandmothers won't find it humorous,
I see it sadly human in such a fuss

To find that single soul key
That hopefully fits the lock of self's identity.

But now we hurry on to meet
The fearless riders with a treat
Of cotton candy for their faces
The best of carnival's good graces.
Forgetting all but having fun.
What better prize could we have won.

God's Love

Blizzard falling on an upstart mountain
Clearing the dizzying air till breath takes hold.
Collecting man's pollutions
Impounding them from him in the cold,
Winter's thinking of his soul.
Spring swirling them to seas secure
Amid unhurried blossoms
Leaving the lakes conserved and pure.

Specific Dyslexia

What purple bordered praetexta
Marks you my child – specific dyslexia?
Difficult, forced, spitting it out
Consonant trickery, vowels un-redeeming.

Meaning more than tongue trickery
Mind stickery – family splittery
Not slow minded – but words
Eyes, hands not complementary.

Child! What genes, what quirk
Of evolution, zigzagging maturity?
Birthright of reading gone half astray
Family foiled; school forced community.
Thou shalt not! How can you say
He's not doing his best today.
Struggle for him, not his enemy dare
To love him as he fights this war.

Perhaps he'll discover in his will to learn
A new understanding, a God not stern
Or quick to chastise weakness –
But growth of mind born high in triumph's meekness.

Waiting at O'Charley's

I always ask for Donnie
Like old times
With my dear one
Who loved the French dip sandwich
Loneliness loves the company
Who shared good quips of humor
With us both
He brings the rolls and
Gives the old widow
An understanding hug
Memories come alive once more
The smile worth waiting for

The Politician

I like your wit and knowledge and your clout
Enough to vote you in and others out
A compromised improvement
Nets the haul
To win them all.

But it takes losing
Or a sense of sin
To find the route
That paves with purity
A rock bed of self-doubt.

Faith

Faith changes what I look for
Faith changes what I see
And what I see changes me.
And I change what used to be
To include all three.

Ill-Placed Period

Black on white ambling cursively
Punctuating your life with the incessant questions
Of his wagging appendage
Quickly forgiving the verbose failures of your answers
With a lick of your hand.

No mindless foot pumping gas
Could articulate such a delicate pause.

Symbols flow turning time into a linear rush
Of computed abstractions.

Meaning crushes definitions
And gives them life
Like the force of an ill placed period.

Tears

Tears were waiting there.
Laughter said they're gone for good –
Love glows with laughter as it should,
No room for tears to share,
But tears were waiting there.

Bliss comes and goes with zeal.
Loves keeps an even keel with smiles,
The guardian of life's journeyed miles
To map all we may feel.
Tears hiding? Are they real?

But you are gone, and laughter flees
And tears no longer hide,
Oh! You were always at my side
Together facing age dis-ease.
Now waiting tears unleash their seas.

The only thought that comforts me –
Oh! Let me know for certain
That behind death's dismal curtain
Your laughter rings for all to see.
A place no tears could ever be!

Windows

Windows help us focus
As does art,
Yet on a changing part
Of all that is our locus.
Beauty is best captured
In elegant small doses.
That is all that God proposes
We can handle of his rapture.

For homework pay attention
To see the shapes they take.
My First Graders never fake
The answers on this mission.

Round ones are a find.
Though oval makes them guess
The world is more or less
A puzzle of some kind.

My favorite is the bay
And when at heaven's door
I'll ask for one thing more
The chance to read one day
In the comfort of a big one.

Trellises

We trellised summer days
With morning porches and mayonnaise crackers
Peeking through safe squares
Gauzing the parched garden
As if filming a crow crossed face
In remembrance of spring grace.

Flat monotony softens in shadows
Danced on wooden planks,
Crossing oblique rhythm
In grosser parallels.
Sunshine patches dazzle us to mirth
Manned with cans we mudpie in the earth.

Trellises date quaint.
Patio patterns focus the scene
With rock hard motion,
All depths to orbit adventure
In current concrete lace,
No shield to hide from space.

I grow seasick empty
Hungering for hidden crosses,
Childhood's trellises
To lay them straight.

A Landscaped Mind

I'm not one
>for pastel picnics

Rainbow dried after spring rain.

>I complain

Of too sudden kindness
>>With unshed tears
>>Hope without words.

I walk away from daisies that leer.

Don't stalk me with spider-web diamonds
>like a lacey sautoir
>or watercress edges
>of bubbling frontiers.

I avoid forests with sun-dappled shadows
>like far away songs
>you cannot quite hear.

My world's too fragile to respond in kind
>the future interest inflated
>in spontaneous soarings
>of a landscaped mind.

Make Us Whole

Is there sickness in each soul
Inaccessible to self-control
Or knife, or word, or will
Of human skill
Or ritual console?

What's left in all the world
To make us whole?

Society

I pull into my cube,
Six squares of alienation.
Not a sphere or tube
Cornered for reconciliation.
Lines that angle back
Flatness that fingers
Grope or hack,
Measured length that lingers
Retrospective calculation.

A door declares it house
Comfort and isolation
Shared with loving spouse.
Decorated in consolation
Limiting beauty
Practicing proximo –
A containing quiet duty
Artful self-dilemma
Compacted confrontation.

Corners, lines, and knobs –
Final invitation,
Clamoring heart throbs,
Draining radiations
Draw me out.
Sideling to comparison
Back inside to pout,
Reluctant revisions.

Shell after shell
Emptying from squares,
Hurrying pell-mell
Encountering dares
Discovering a Heaven
And a Hell.

Box Hockey at West Park

The crossed sticks of two young wills opposed
Over the poised puck, their world compacted in its globe
Ready to be rent from its planked perch.

Sun browned bodies flanking the détente
Fearless of the frenzy of the box.

Two ways out, and one must declare itself forsaken
If one declares itself fulfilled.
Poise, click, check, click
The sticks fly with the wills.

One mighty tingling coordination flows through to thrust,
Hold back, then share the moment of unchecked.
Crowd murmurs roll the rules along
To ward off wild intent.
The winning stroke surprises the loser in a smack of defeated inches.

No winners gloating time
Just a steeling of grip for the next encounter.

It hours away the endless summer
For children waiting in bunches
The promise of free box lunches
Cold war heroes
Impulsively playing their hunches.

Just a game when they all walk away.

Summer Flu

What to do
For the summer flu,
High on Bio-C
And Coryban-D.
Squirming and aching
Sneezing and shaking.
The reading endeavor
Though not all that clever
Mortifies days
Of juices and sprays.
Old <u>TIMES</u> come to life
With their comical strife
Through a feverish daze
Reversing the haze,
Telescopes their clarity
Ego sine charity.
The government wins
For humor and sins,
Congressional morals
Receiving prize laurels.
At least their crass
Makes good news – not their class.
But not all that's banal
Is oral or anal
Some of its typed
Might better be wiped.

The Death of a Child

The fog that shrouds our faith
The gray blanket that suffocates our spirit.
Why?
Why, God?
No answer,
No answer we are ready to hear.
Punishment?
My God would not punish that way,
He gives life, He gives it with abundant love.
Chance?
That seems even harder to take.
Freedom?
The price of freedom.
Say some more.
The gray is for groping.
Room to grow.
Happiness and tragedy are two of the teachers.
Neither can teach alone.

But the aching, oh the ache!
It will be comforted.
The life so short –
The things missed?
Love is eternal
One moment of love is forever.
The opposite of love is emptiness.

I would have gone in their place.
I would gladly have gone.
For one or two or perhaps a nation
Christ went for all of us.
He covered all the gray with love.

He reached across the freedom.
He carried love across the chasm.
We walk the bridge He built.
There was no knowledge of happiness like His knowledge,
There was no ache like His ache.

Walk around in your freedom.
Business as usual?
No, take this new knowledge,
Take the light of love into the grayness.
Reach as far as you can across the chasm.
Love each other more than ever.
It will answer all the questions,
Blot out all the blame,
Lead our paths through the grayness.

Life is not for hate, guilt, or blame,
They are nothing.
Life is for love.
Love cannot hurt, hate, blame, destroy.
Love is for eternity.

Aunt Dorothy's House

Smell of antique wood, rubbed, sanded
Smoother, brighter than before,
Meeting walnut, oak, and maple at their core
With toil, not stain, applied strong handed.
Who seeks, loves, polishes something old,
Speaks continuity from nature to man's will,
The forest art to help repel the chill
Before the hordes of men came uncontrolled.

From piece to piece I go to trace
Each wood grain lightly sealed.
Growth hidden as it happened – now revealed
As beauty reverenced, power, and grace.
Tables, chairs, oak desk with scrolls,
The stool goes round and round
For children still. The years compound
The learning as life's mysteries unroll.

The family framed in silent smiles,
Portraits of children who bring their own
Families on occasion, to share, atone
For linkages they lost across the miles.
Husband, parent's faces also stare
As if from their eternal place
They try to life love upward into space
In memory of a time of mortal care.

Clocks chiming bring me back to time.
So do the smell of mace and dill,
Business as usual in the kitchen mill,
Company keeps it always in its prime.
Collector's glass radiates the table

Nourished in linen as a preparation
For the feast itself – divine temptation
Making self-denial a forgotten fable.

Aunt Dorothy shares contentment in her lore,
An inner-shined and polished light,
Showing life's rough edged gritty might
Some hard and solid store.

Kitchen

I've wrapped myself in my new, old kitchen
Black and white with a silver bow.
A gift – rather no dishwasher
Then live with another's grimy show.

Black paisley over the rail
Rhythmically stamped on silver foil
Topping black poles on white
Well-turned soldiers in row-some toil.

White tiled counter checkered straight
Asking chessmen what they ate.
Silvered steel in stove and oven
Cookiemen march to an even dozen.

Cupboards the black knights
Marbleized medallions centered white
Oval shields reflecting the flow
From pierced tin lantern glow
Thousand speckled dancing light.

If I were rich? A decorator
Would design it all from new.
Poor? Pictures, dreams, and potato stew.

No imagination can make me
Misfit, rebel, retarded,
But bring them on in for it's well guarded.

Single? Once – washing dishes, too.
And teaching children who
Can't speak or hear as well as you.

Purpose, facts, self, beauty?
How to know one's honest duty?

A man? The young ones say
They can do anything a man can.
Preach sermons, fight wars
Build kitchens everyday
Some to be eight months pregnant in the plan.

But for me, now
I've wrapped myself in lace
Silver, paisley and how
To give love here a place.

Forget your muddy feet
The white floor needn't be so neat,
Come talk to me while I do the dishes
Pass the time exchanging wishes.

A Christmas Bag

I carried tardy gifts to neighbors
In a bag emptied of torn clothes
For the job. Christmas eve labors
Weigh as light as those last leaves the evening blows
Before it settles down in a cold, still wait.
Wind and cold enough to make cheeks red,
For Santa's job – a noble Santa trait.
A walking one this time – no snow or sled.

The first two families busy as my own
About the business of Christmas customs kept,
Ribbons, whispers, doors, cakes, monotone
Of sheer delight at which we're all adept
This special night. A smile and we all know
The melting together of our merriment.
We speak the spoken customs and I go,
Bag, one from empty, their gifts already sent.

I saved this one for last. It is her job
To sell today as any full day's work
For overtime you meet the Christmas mob
Or stay home poorer, if you're a widow clerk.
I set the bag down as I rang the bell,
Then got the only package left inside.
As if I had released some magic spell
A whirl of wind and shopping bag complied,
The one container, the other one control
To fly the porch wall and escape together.
So quick, no chance to reason or cajole
And strangely felt stranded by some paper.

The light had startled my still stare
Some seconds before I focused on my friend.
Smiling, she ushered me to my usual chair
Where, listening mostly, had helped us both to mend.
"Open it now," I'd said just like a child,
And handed her the package that I held.
Picking up my tempo, a little wild,
Ripping ribbon and paper until she was compelled
To squeal with laughter and almost cry.
An antique box with Limoges butterflies.
I'd splurged not really knowing why
Till this crescendo of our shared surprise.
Its proffered usefulness doubtful at best,
But beauty leaps when least expected
To fill the mind with a moment's rest.
We all have need to be disconnected
From the going on of our everydayness.
Without it we grow blindly cold
To everything we cannot label progress
And fit it into some gigantic mold.

We settled down at last to conversation.
Tomorrow she would drive to see her son.
I thought I heard behind her explanation
Needs of families sometimes to be alone.
Late, like me, she had just wrapped our present
For the whole family, so I left it wrapped,
Said our best wishes and I went content.
Outside remembering I had mapped
The course my shopping bag might follow
If the wind died soon after their departure.
Close by I searched a grassy hollow
Up and down vainly, leaving all to nature.

It had served me well its stay,
Once sitting by a lonely friend to give
Some books and hope and listen to me pray
In silence that her dreams might live.
In summer it took a tomboy's change of jeans
To a country picnic glowing in the sun;
The jeans had turned to rocks by dubious means
When back home late and tired we brought our fun.
Tonight it went from rags to porcelain,
From a closet it escaped on Christmas wings
And if tomorrow someone uses it again
It can remember carrying all these things.

No butterfly cocoon falls from me
To reveal a flight of fancies color
For one ephemeral season. I will be
The sack instead. Laugh with me together
And call me an old bag,
Who, come Christmas Eve, empties gifts
And burdens and every forgotten rag
Until a vacuum remains. Christmas Peace lifts
On the winds and fills the hollow corners
Of all this emptiness with cheer.
Begin again with all the laughers, workers, mourners,
Sackless, to carry any load this year.

On Christmas Eve a spirited sack can try
The uncharted updrafts, like a butterfly.

Vacation?

By any other name my nose
Could not smell lavender or rose
At castle, cairn, or lifts
Ol' Janie was the one with sniffs.

Vacation shouldn't be the place
For coughing, sneezing, aching face.
England call me back once more
When I can see you shore to shore.

These last six poems were written when I was in college.

Wine?

Wine should lift you and elate
'Gainst gravity to compensate.
Wine that's weak and watered down
Leaves you safely on the ground.

Love like wine at your command
Elevates to comprehend
Moving sweetly over lips
Tingles to your fingertips.
If it falls flat on its face
It isn't "wine" in any case.

Love

When my heart is weary of you
Set my eyes to crying
For if my heart is weary of you
My soul is dying.

Innocence

Is innocence blinded with a bright cold
Like suns approaching yet icy bold?
In frozen blue announced campaign
Foreshadowed Doppler shift of pain.
Choose well the dreams you want to keep
They last forever as you sleep.
For love might not remain
If we had ever chosen shame.

Weeds

Sometimes I think I spend my hours
Growing weeds instead of flowers.
Maybe I should go away and
Let them have the final say.
Is it all just too much trouble?
An aching back from bending double!
But then I see the glowing red
As zinnias fill the flower bed.
And cone flowers of every shade
As bright as any school parade.
They fill the eye with pleasantness
Enjoying every breezed caress.

Then light and shadow catch my eye
Like a question from a thoughtful sky.
Do weeds mirror my reflection?
The struggle for beauty and perfection
Against some inner misdirection?

It becomes a different place
Shining with work and grace
Pull them with a gentle hand
As God would always understand,
For without Him we could never seed
Some flowers midst that common weed.

Lament of Lachesis

We reveled like a happy Italy
Awoke to see her star-crossed lovers met
In an open devotion – their red hearts free
Of the rusted wound of tragical regret.

The white intention of nuptial expression
Froze their eyes on the altar bow,
And led their fearful passage to the one
Sweet kneeling of their promised vow.

They set up willingly in a faithful flat.
And ill divining the fuse of true love slacks
Its zeal with an untimely spat
Shy in their privacy, we turned our backs.
Bruised in unfair use the love apple
Crushed to curiosity and was at once
Domestic fruit and prankster's playful
Thrust at inconstancy or churlish dunce.

Without rehearsal the bride, groom, and we
The suspects of a spleened intent
Perform un-applauded tragedy
Of inconspicuous argument.

Someone's Gift

Someone gave me a precious gift
But I turned it quickly away.
I thought I'd have to give in like kind,
It was more than I wanted to pay.

Someone gave my brother the gift
And he took it, though he shared my grief.
He gave it in love for all mankind
As he died on a cross like a thief.

Someone gave me a gift in a last try
And I meekly follow the lead.
If I share with another to open his prize
I've fulfilled the giver's one need.

About Jane Criley Denney

The family dog Frosty enjoys affection from a young Jane.

I was born in 1933 during the Depression. That and the fact that my brother was nine years older gave me the idea that I may have been something of a surprise. Surprise or not, I was raised with loads of love. I got to go to Vanderbilt University on a scholarship (family couldn't afford tuition) and graduated *magna cum laude*. A speech and hearing center had just come to Nashville. Always liking "newness," I took extra courses so I could become a public-school speech and hearing therapist.

Walter Criley and I married right out of college, but I worked for ten years before I quit and had my daughter Marnie. Later, I had a four-month miscarriage. As Marnie grew, volunteer jobs took a lot of my time. My major in college had been English, and I have included some college poems. Not included are grammar school poems about war and junior high poems attempting to be funny.

Marnie went to Missoula, Montana, for college graduate work in environmental studies. She met and married Mark Vander Meer.

They do conservation work there. Her dad, Walter Lockwood Criley, had been Director of Planning for the Tennessee Department of Conservation. He died of cancer at age 54. The visitor center at Radnor Lake State Park is named in his honor as the Walter Criley Visitor Center. Later, I married Jean Stone Denney, Business Manager for the Department of Conservation. His first wife had died of cancer. He died at age 91. My poetry is sometimes religious, questioning, feeling, but often tries to define "love" by words, encounters, and maybe even divisions.

www.ingramcontent.com/pod-product-compliance
Lightning Source LLC
Chambersburg PA
CBHW070857050426
42453CB00012B/2244